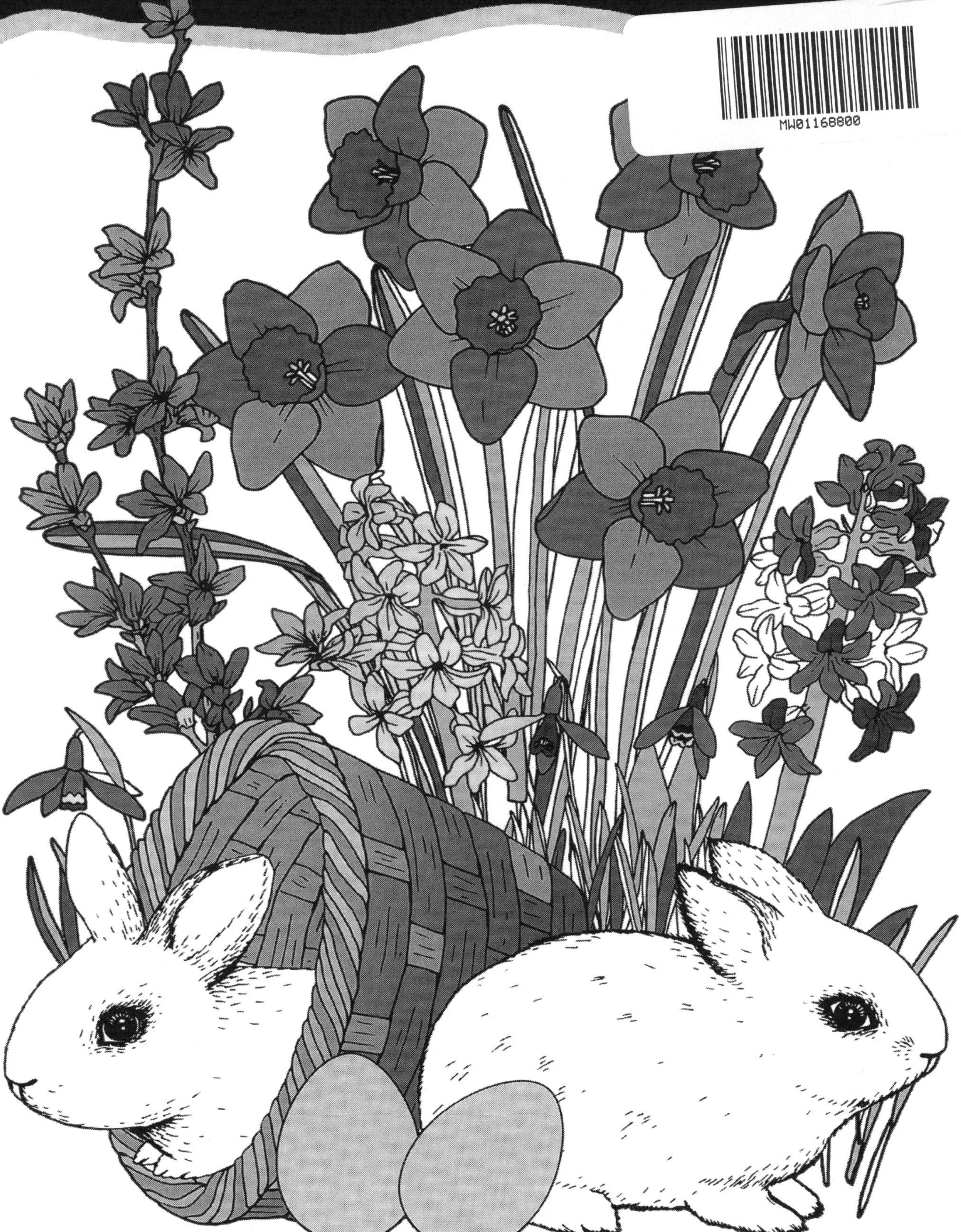

SIMPLE

Coloring Books for Seniors

UNICORN COLORING

Printed in U.S.A.

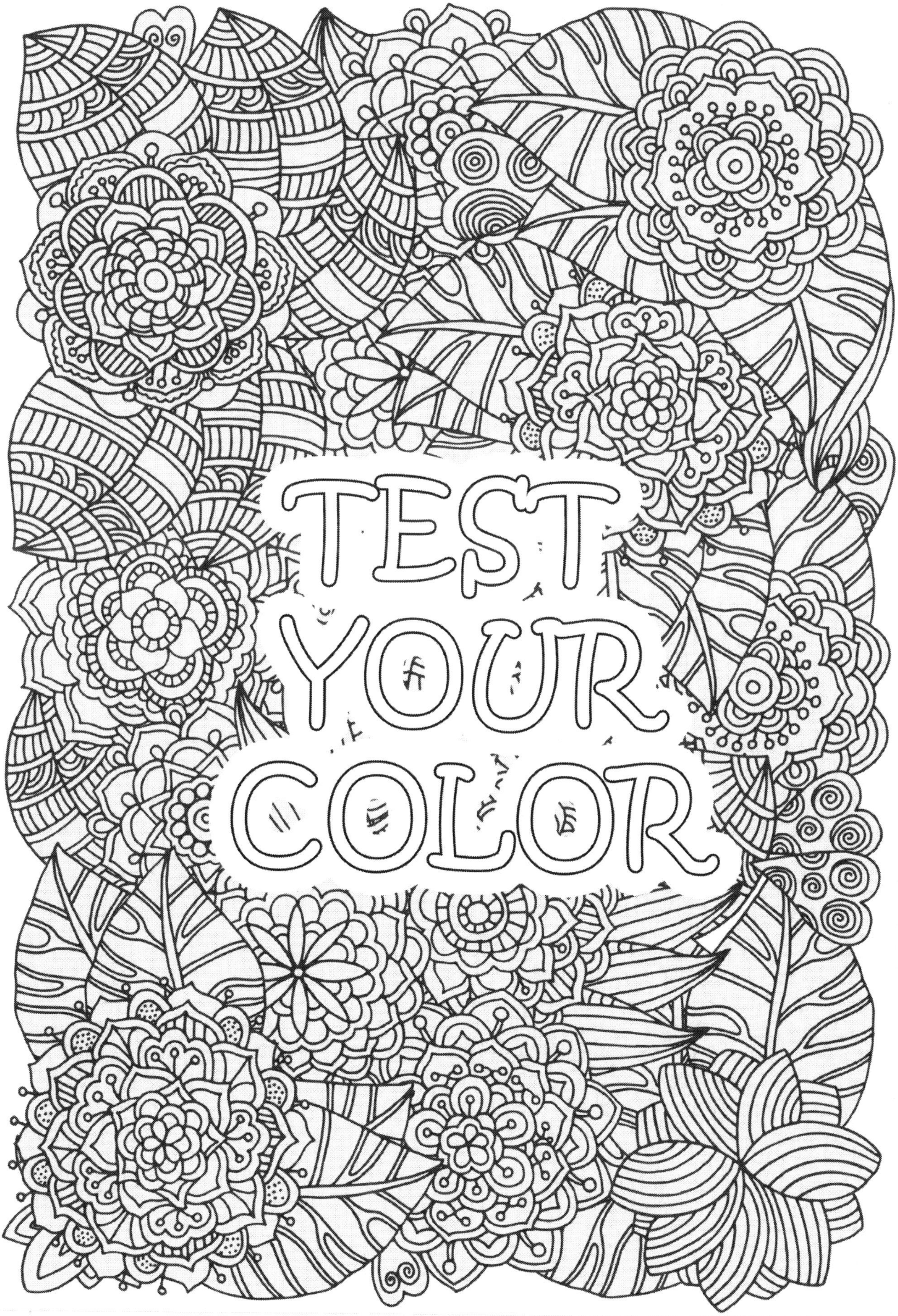
TEST
YOUR
COLOR

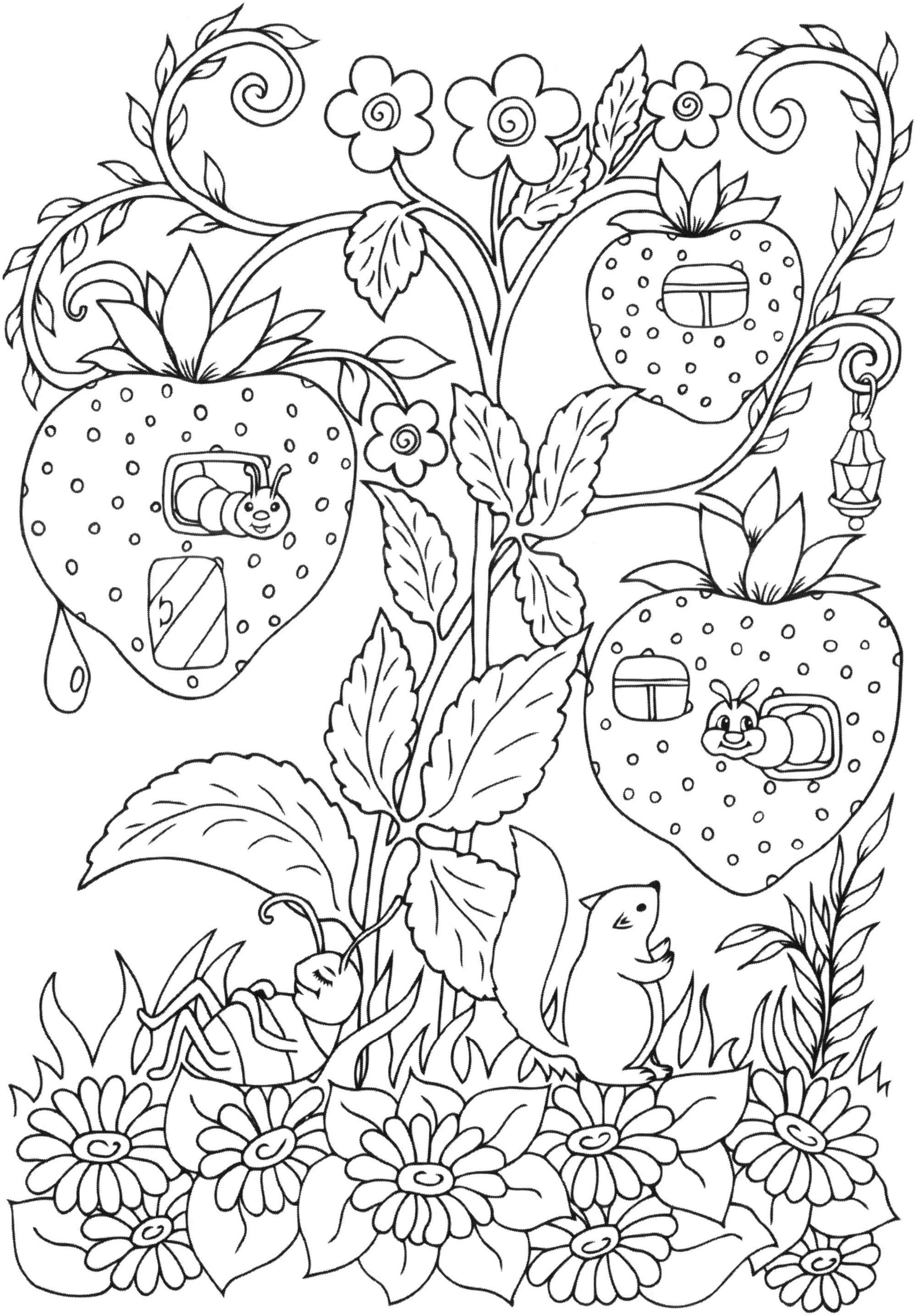

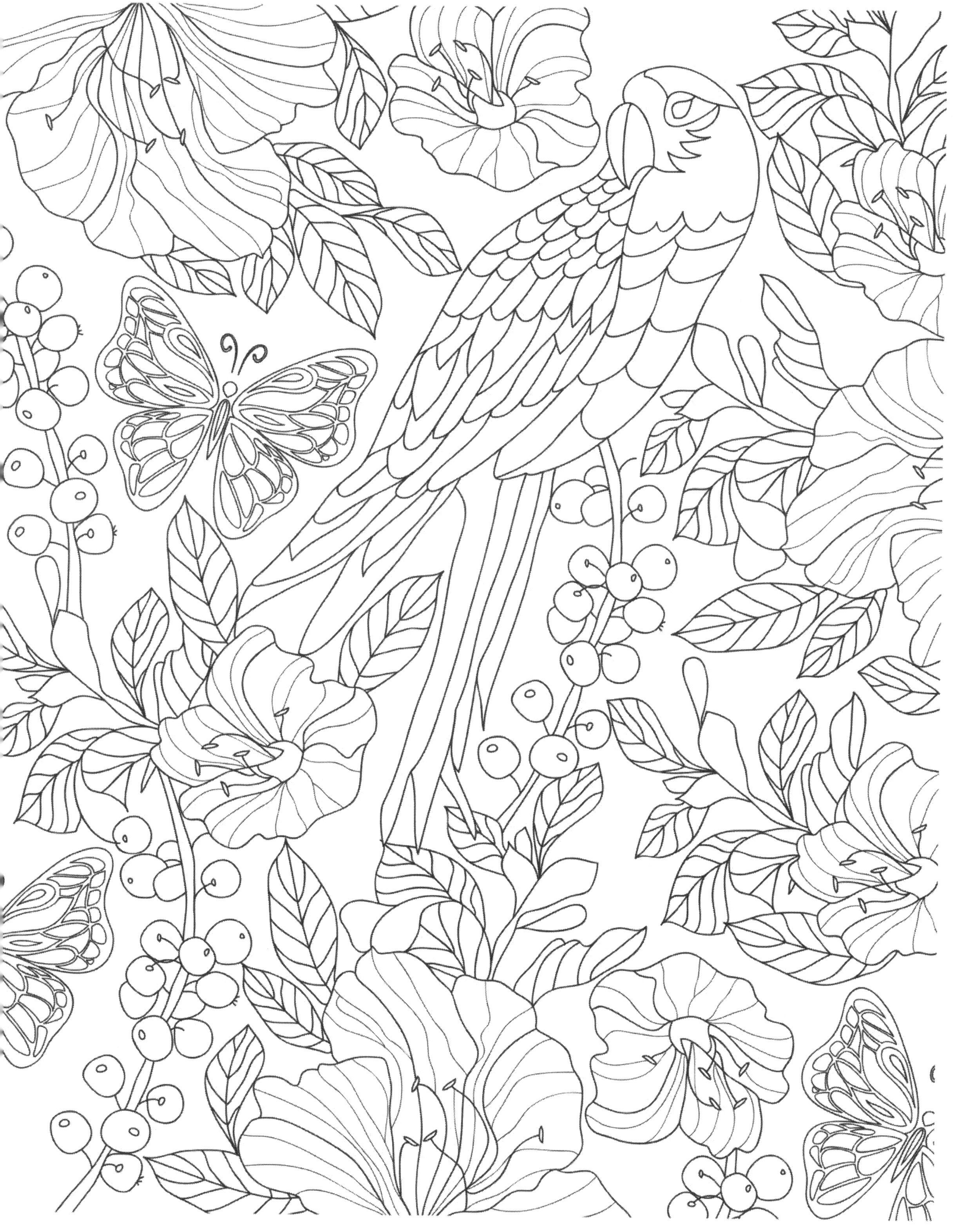

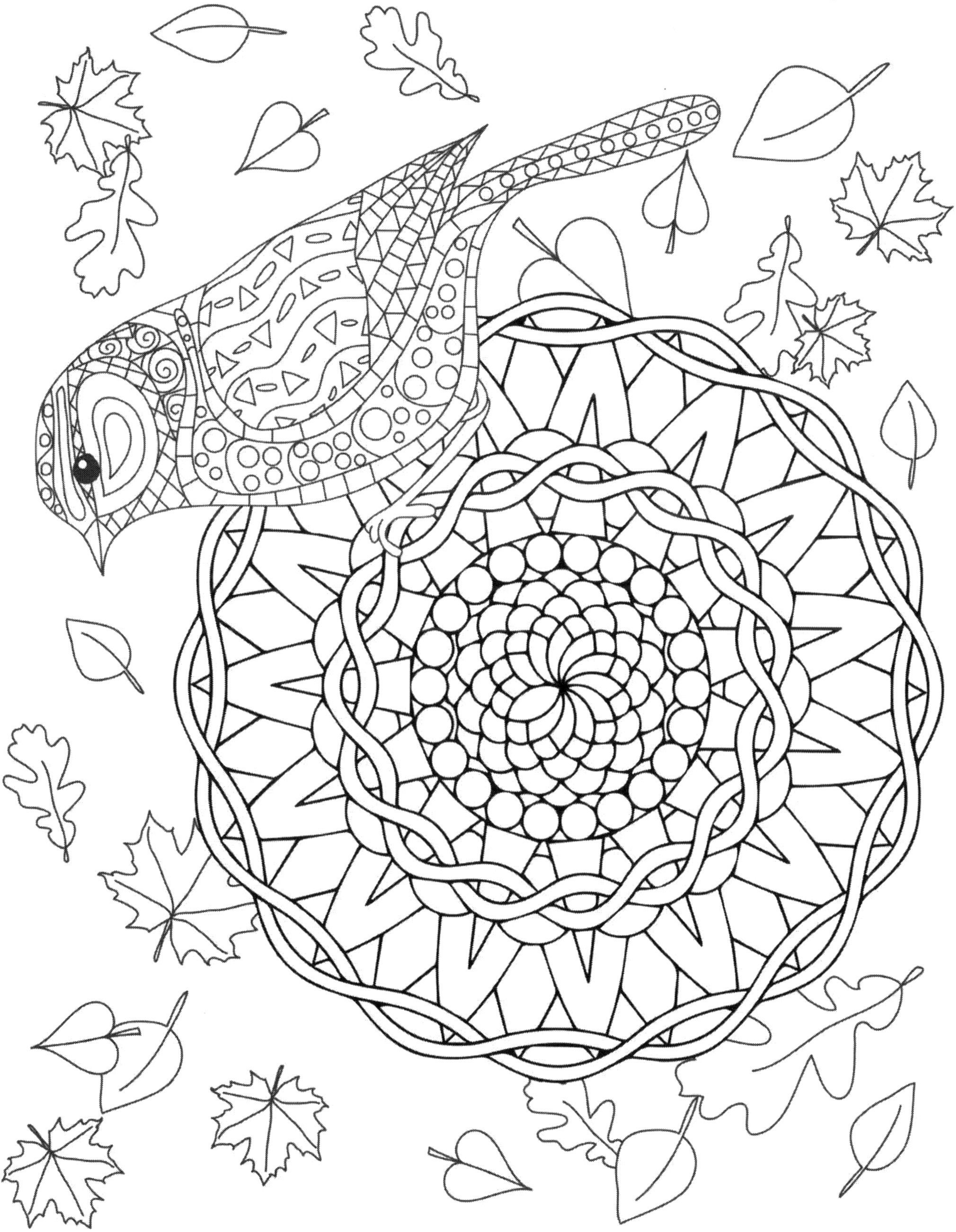

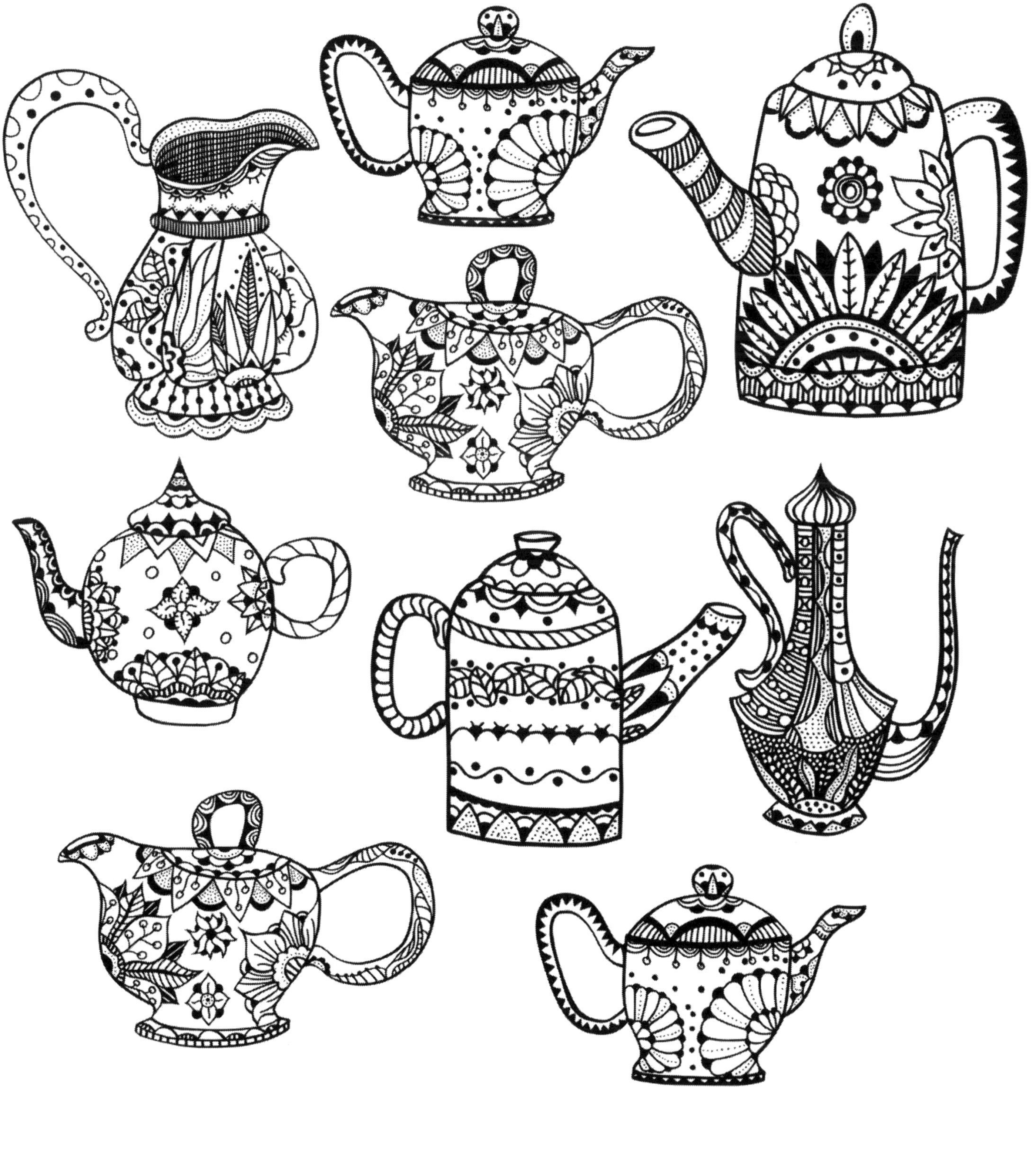

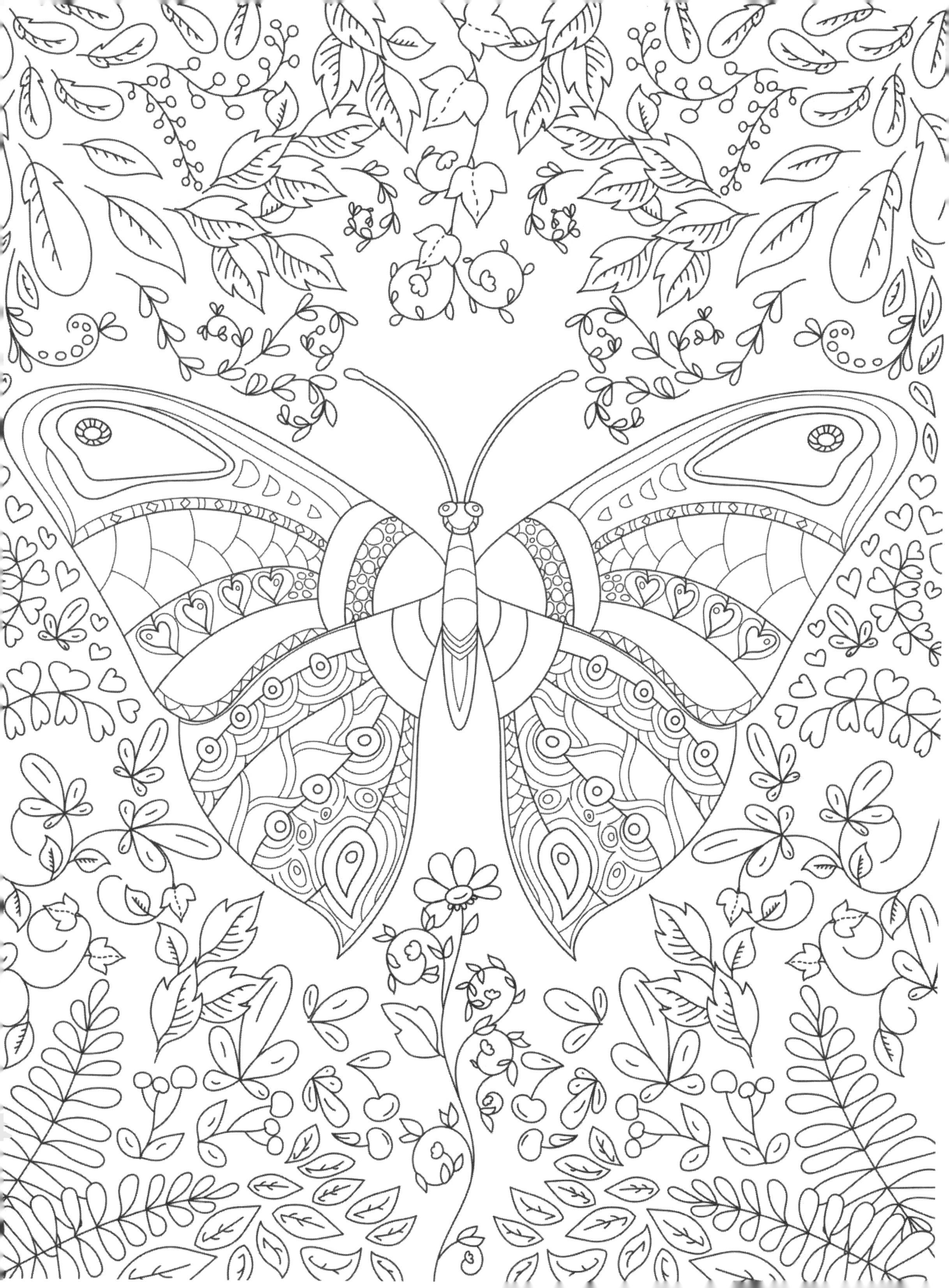

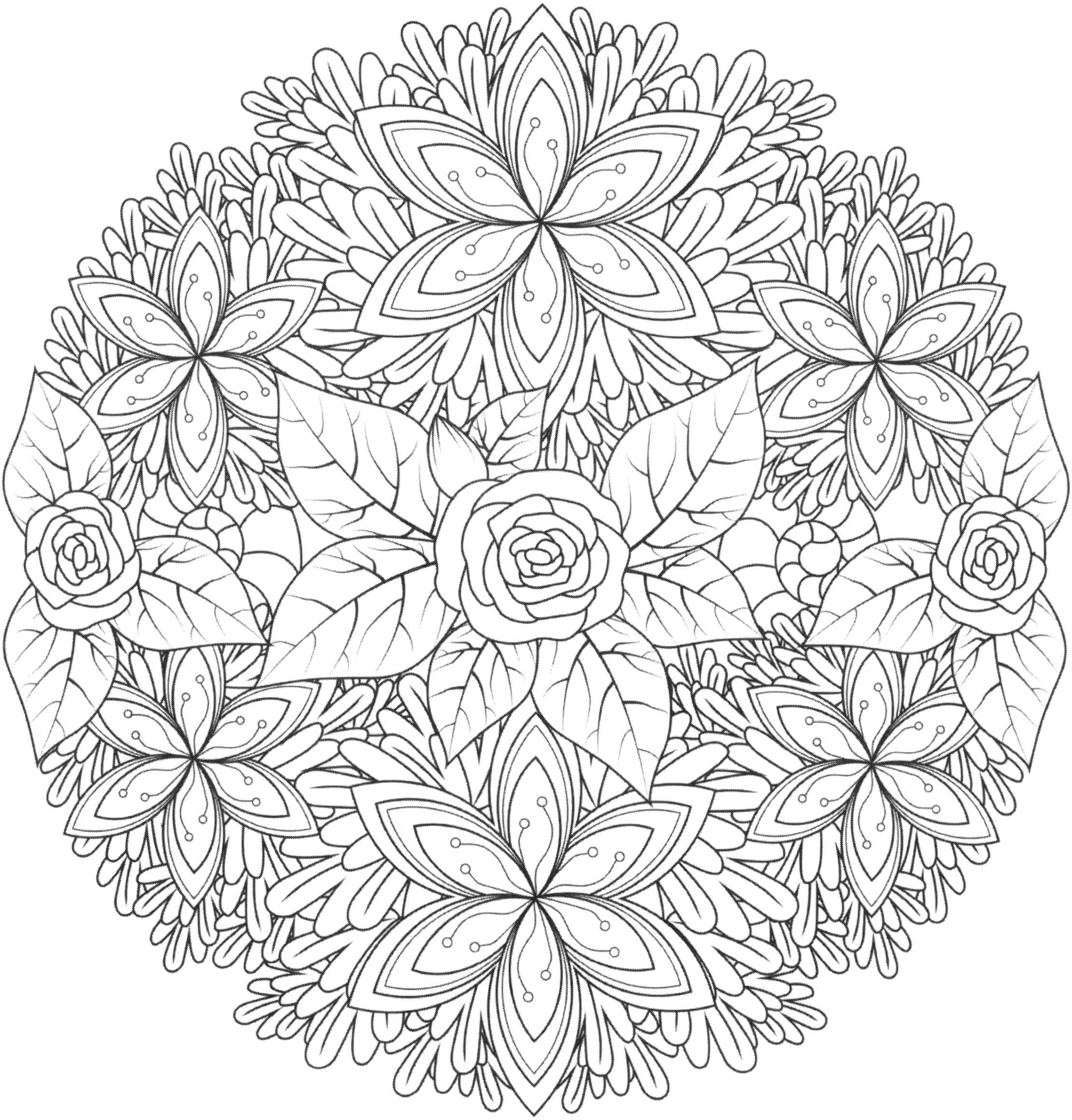

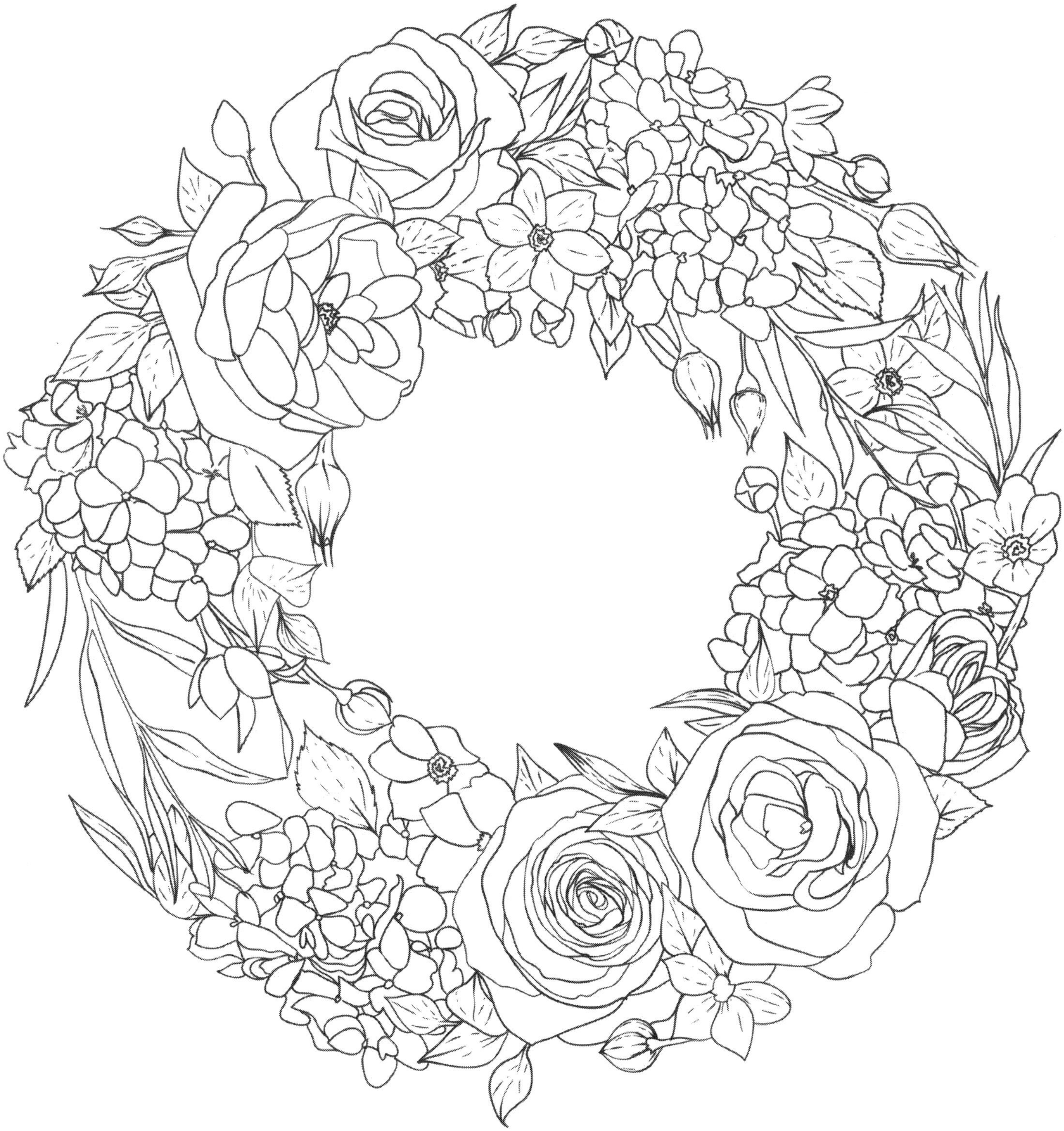

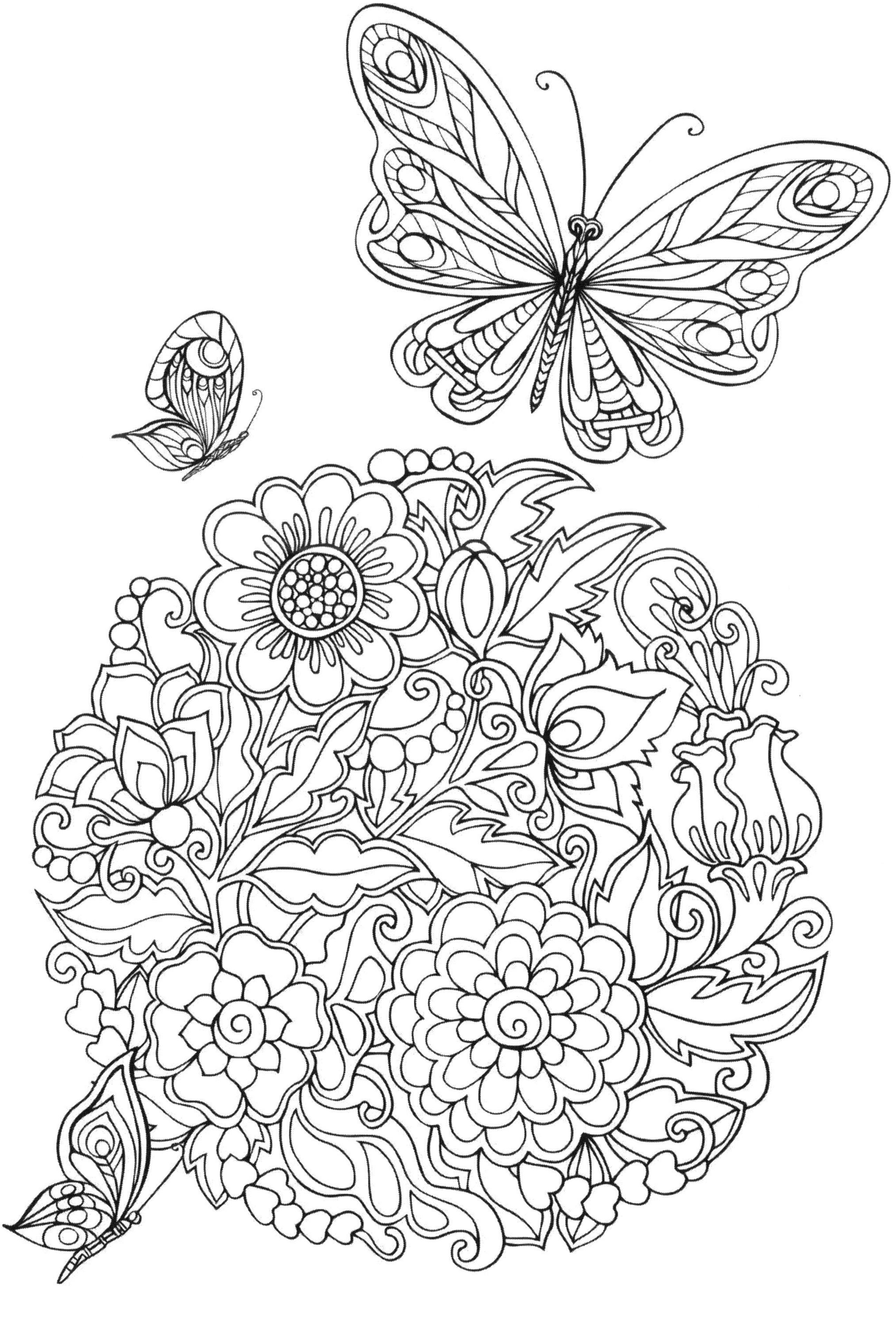

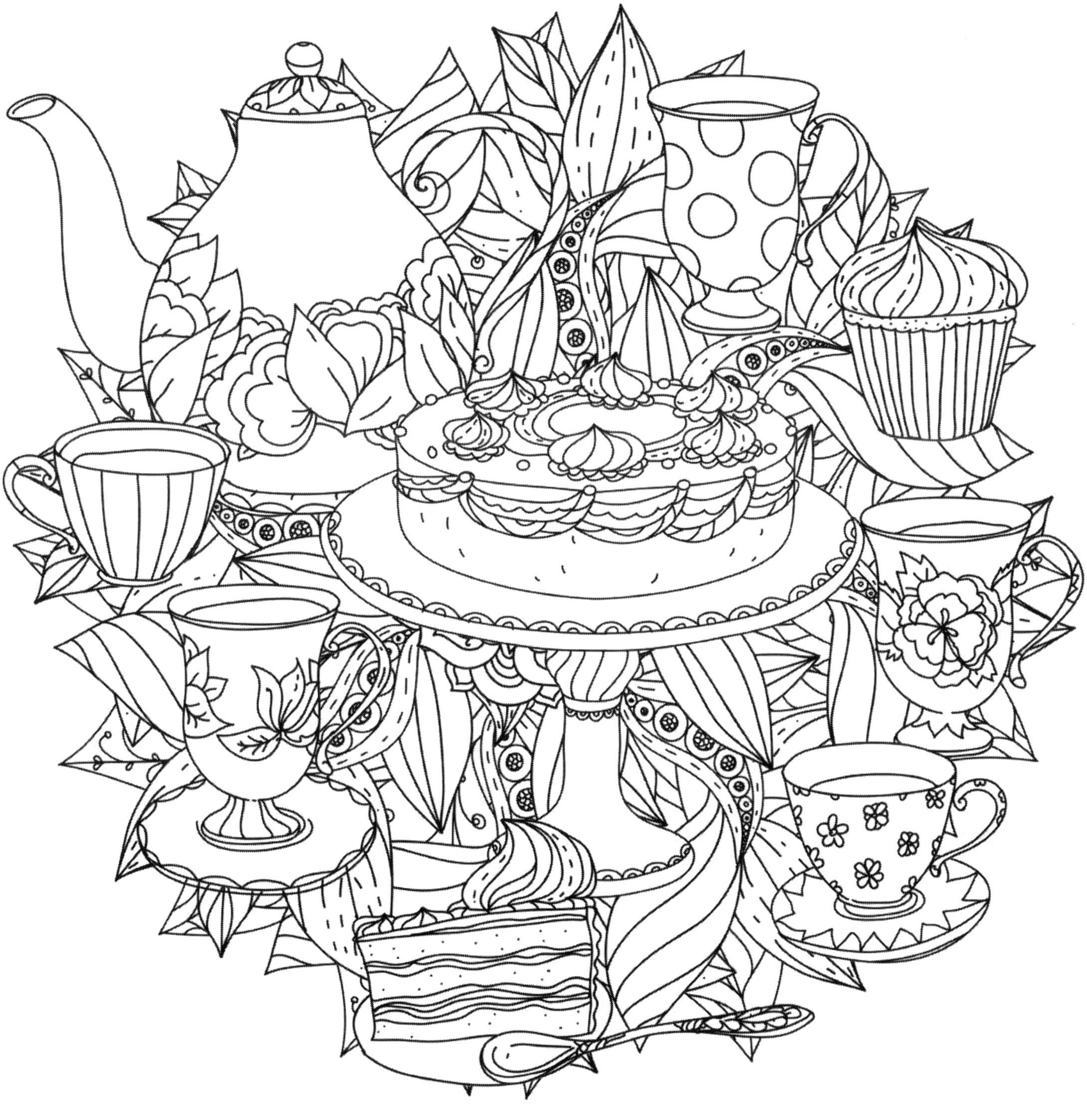

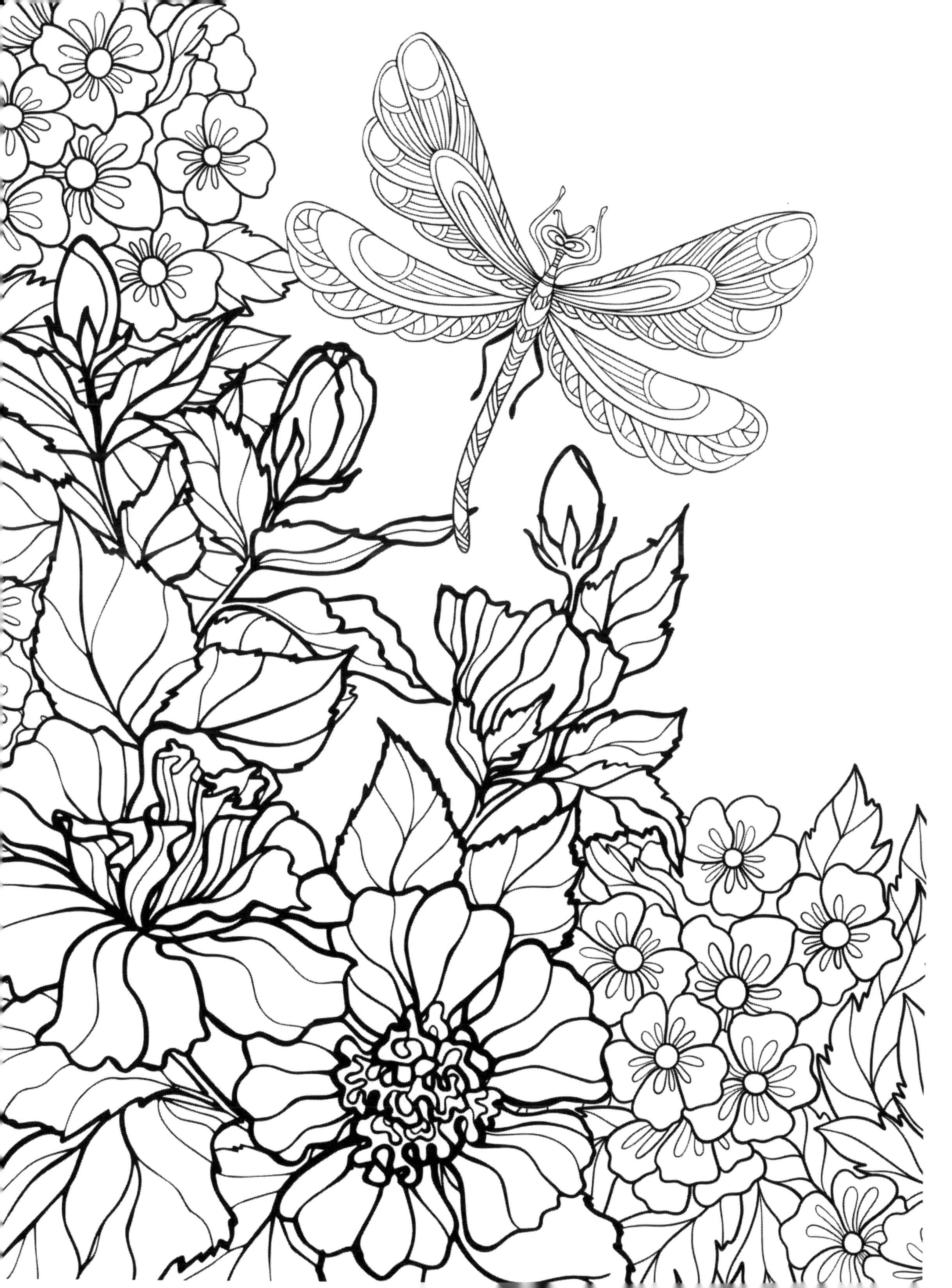

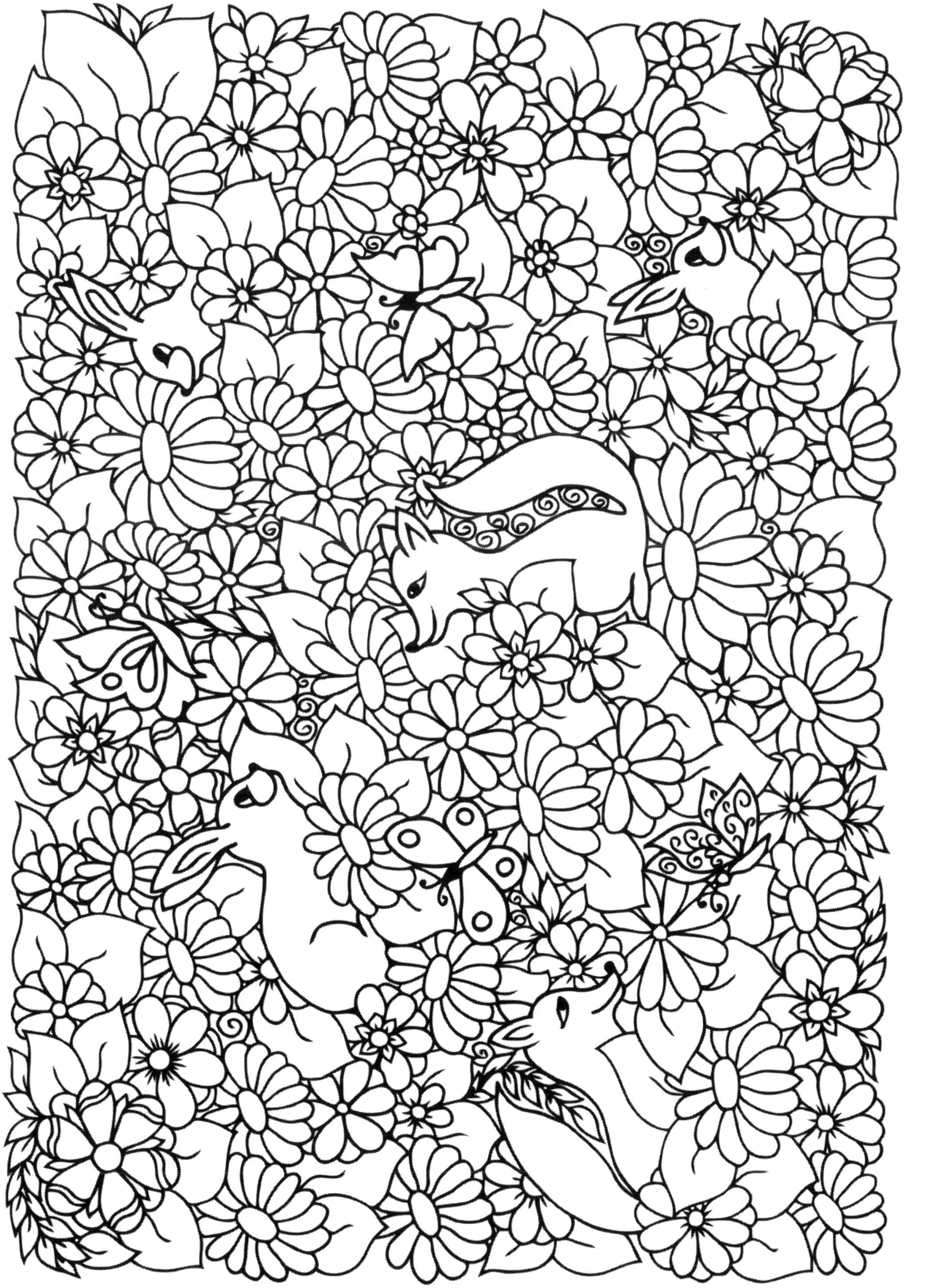

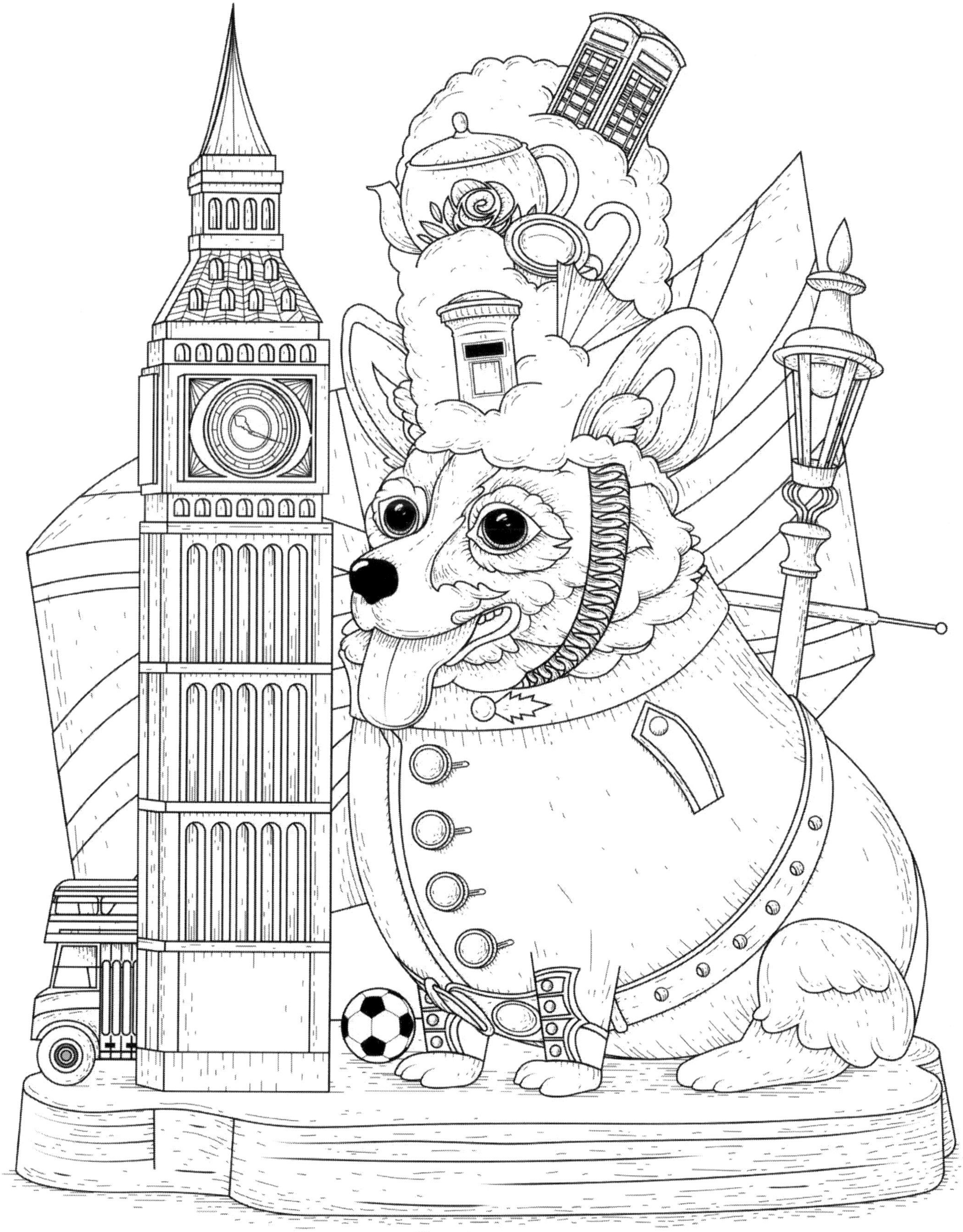

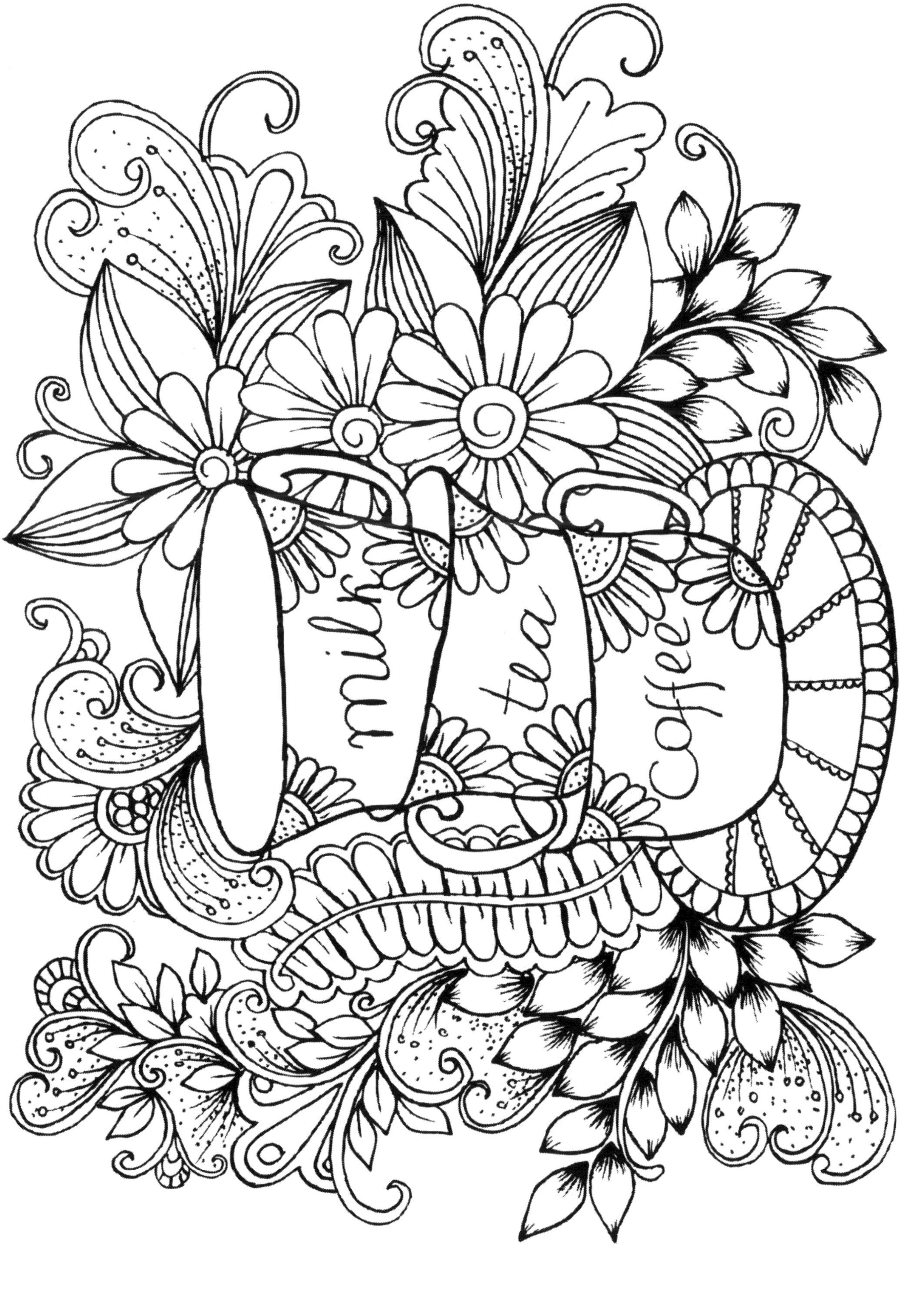
milk
tea
coffee

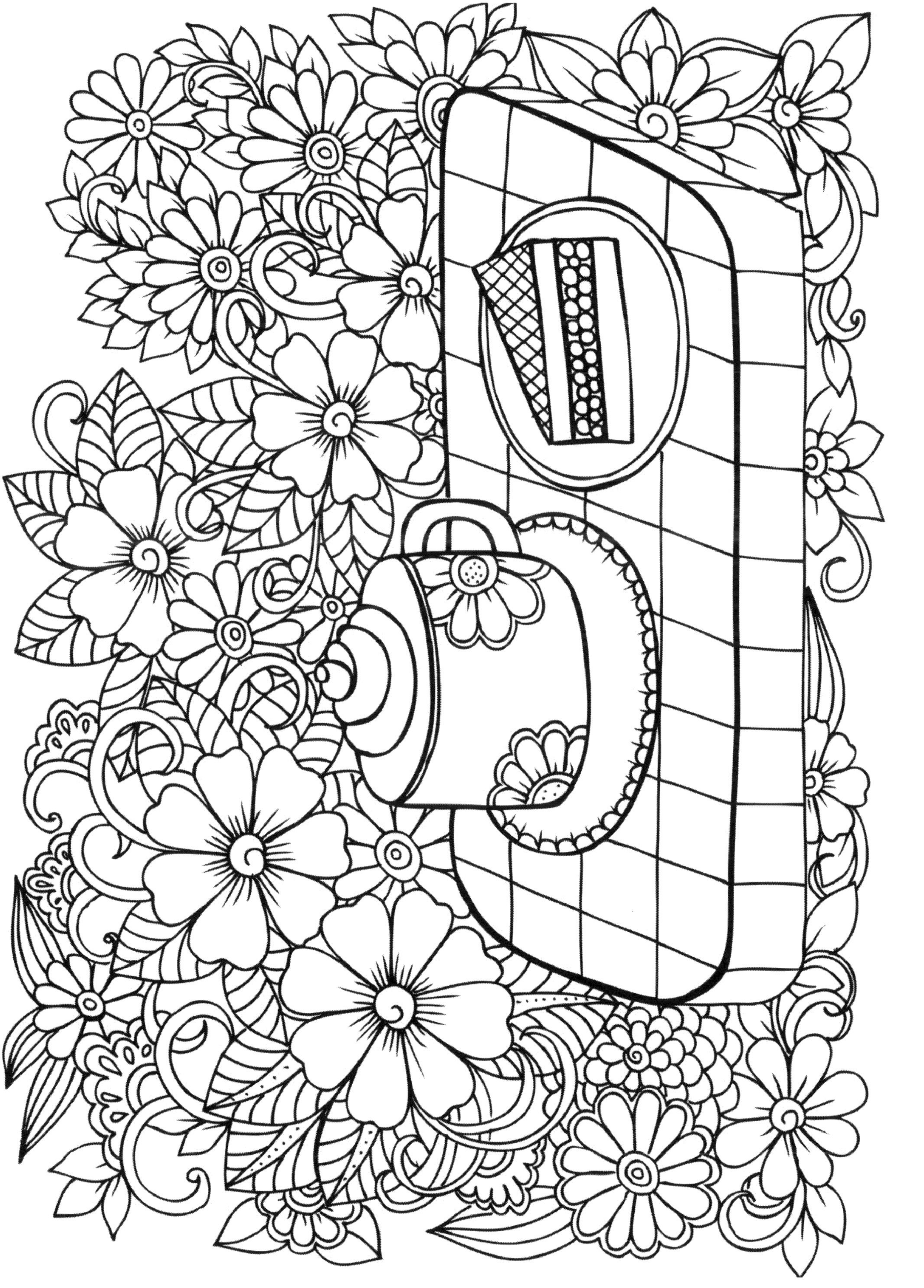

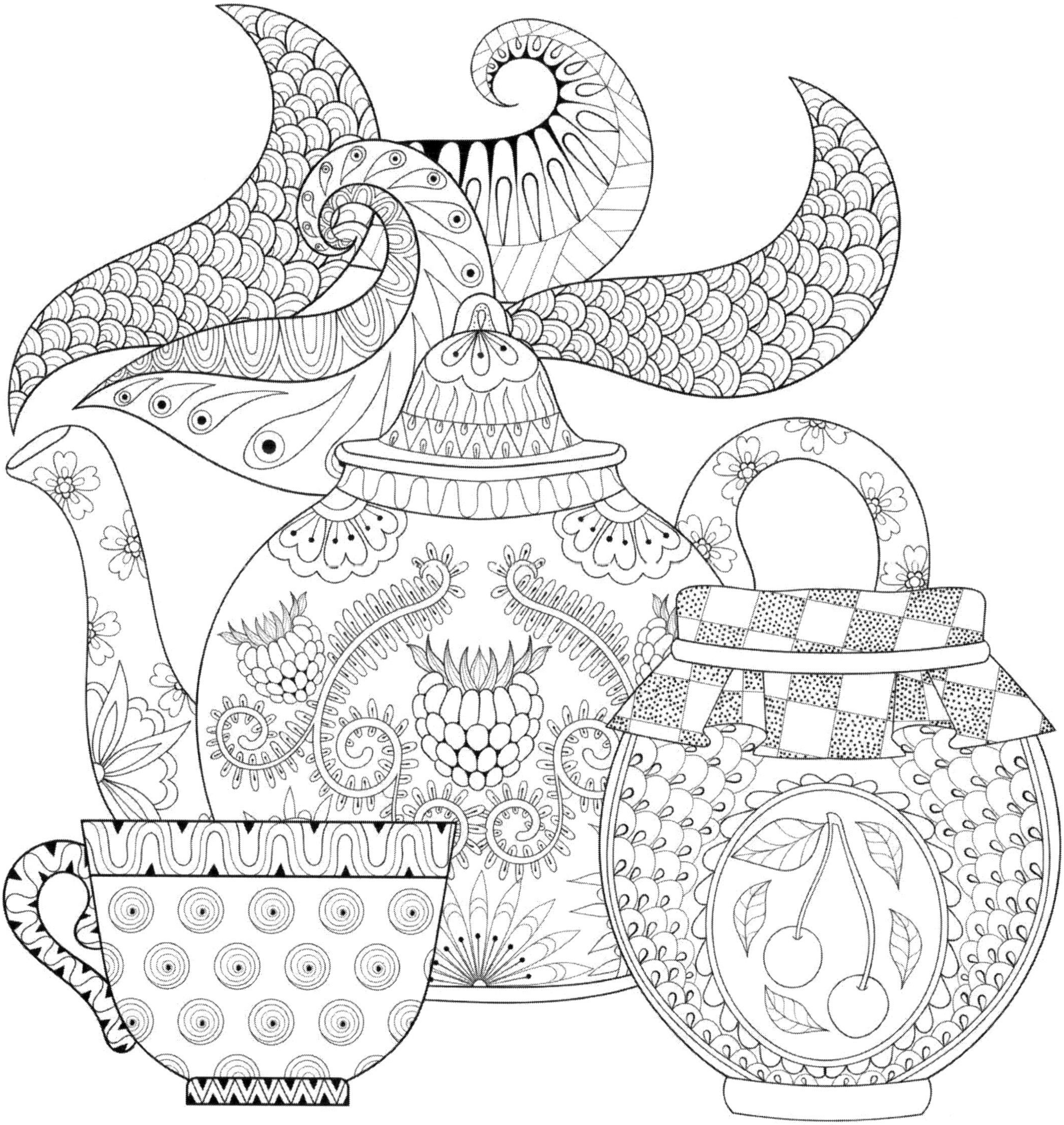

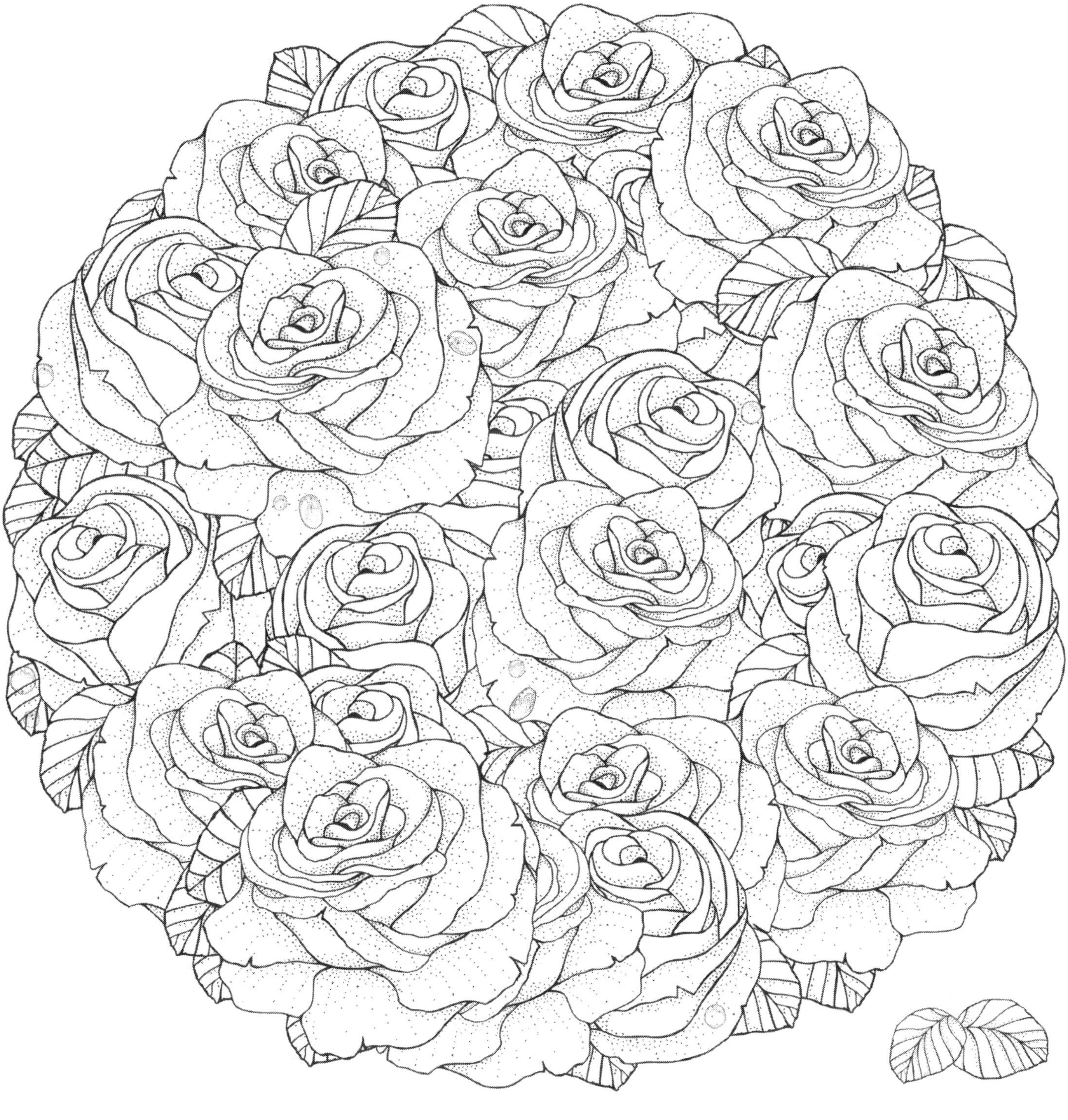

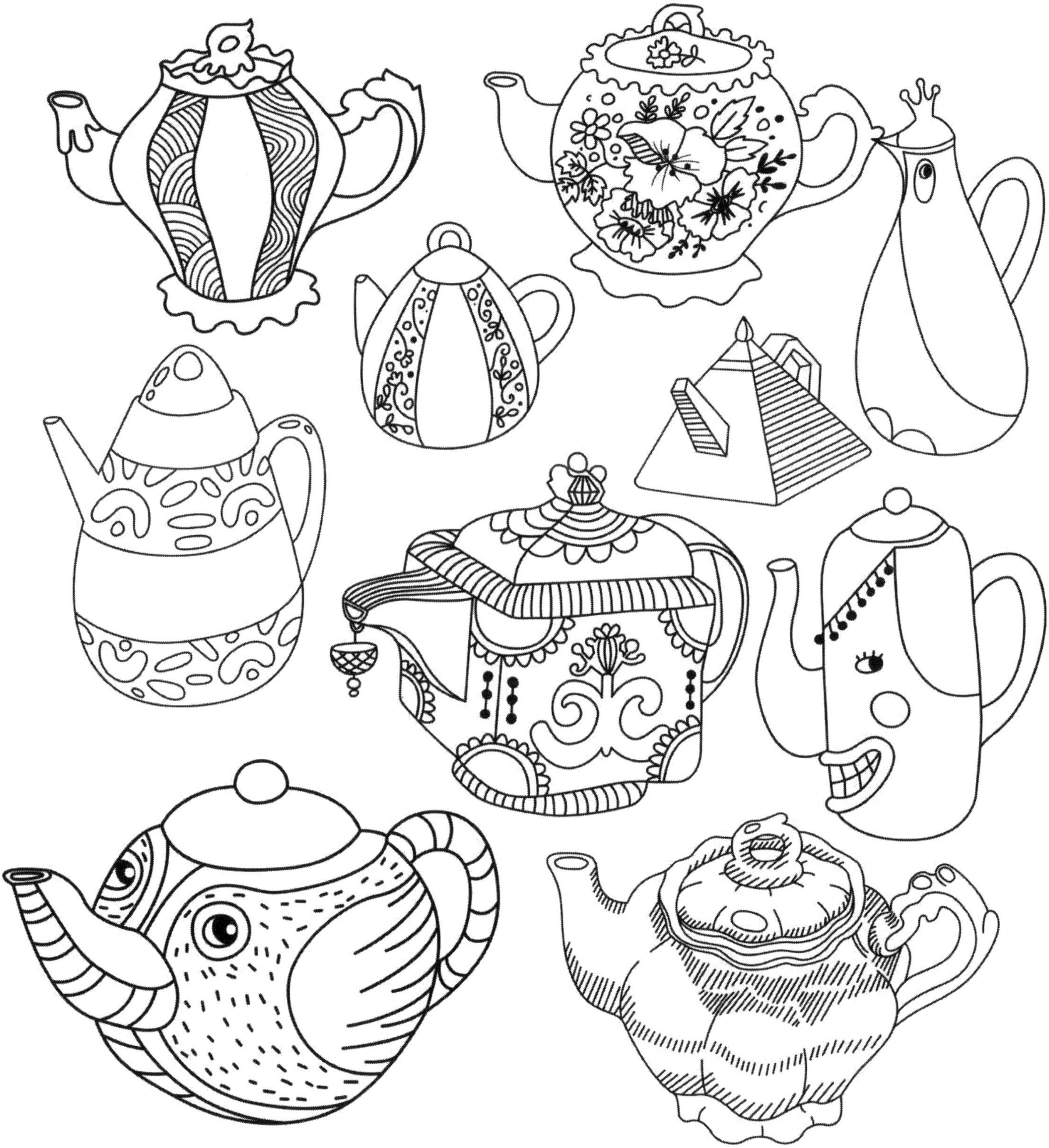

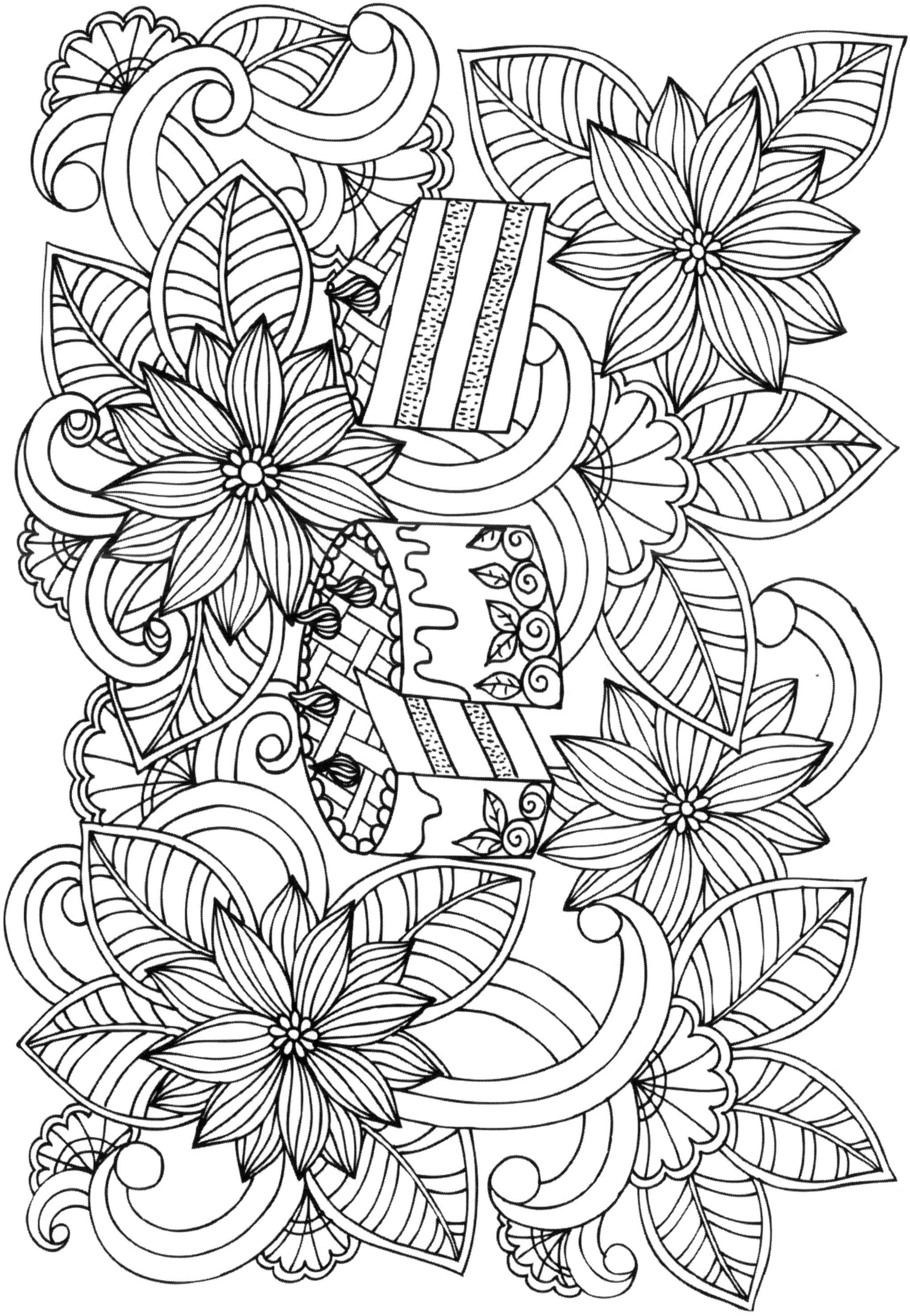

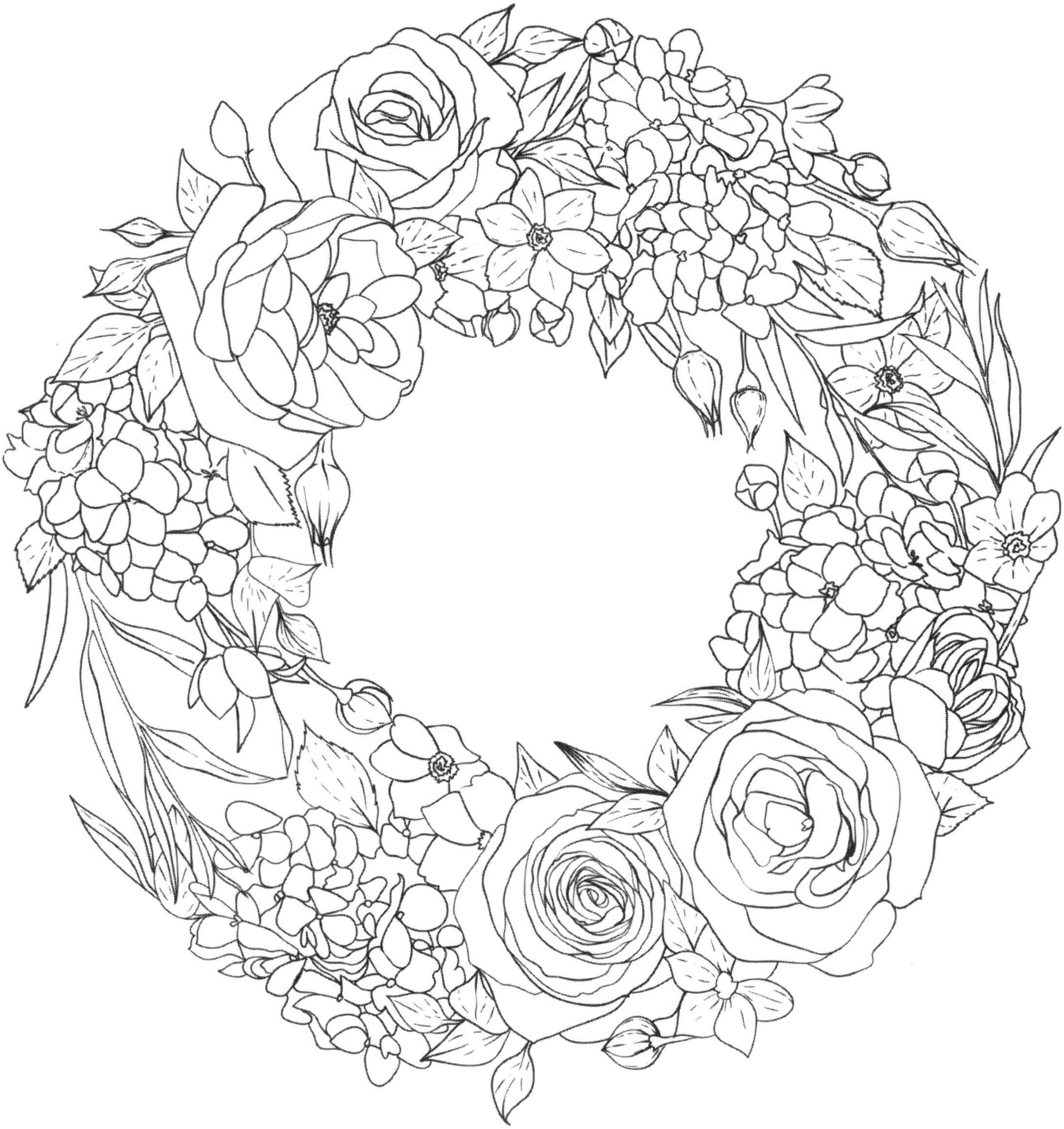

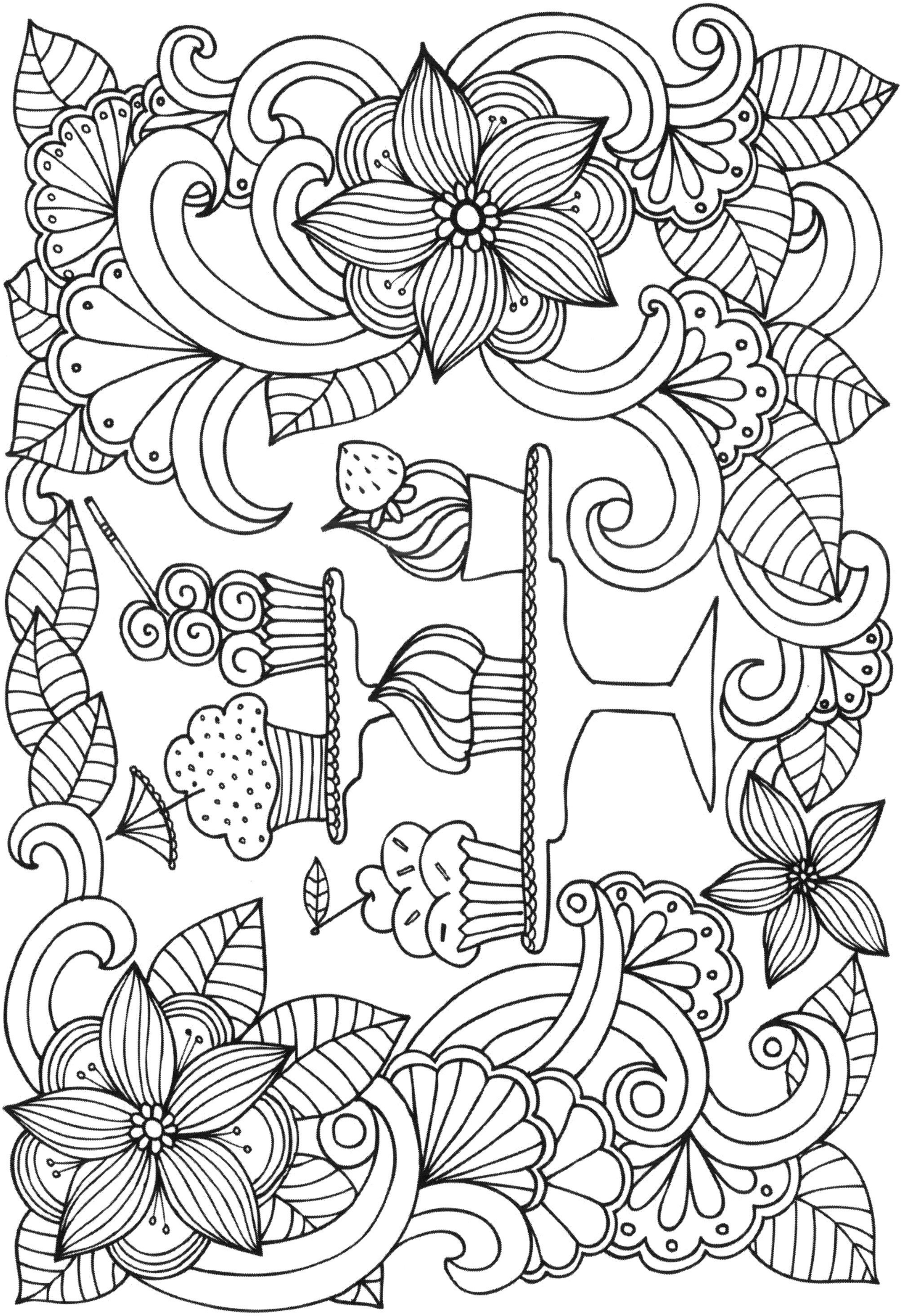

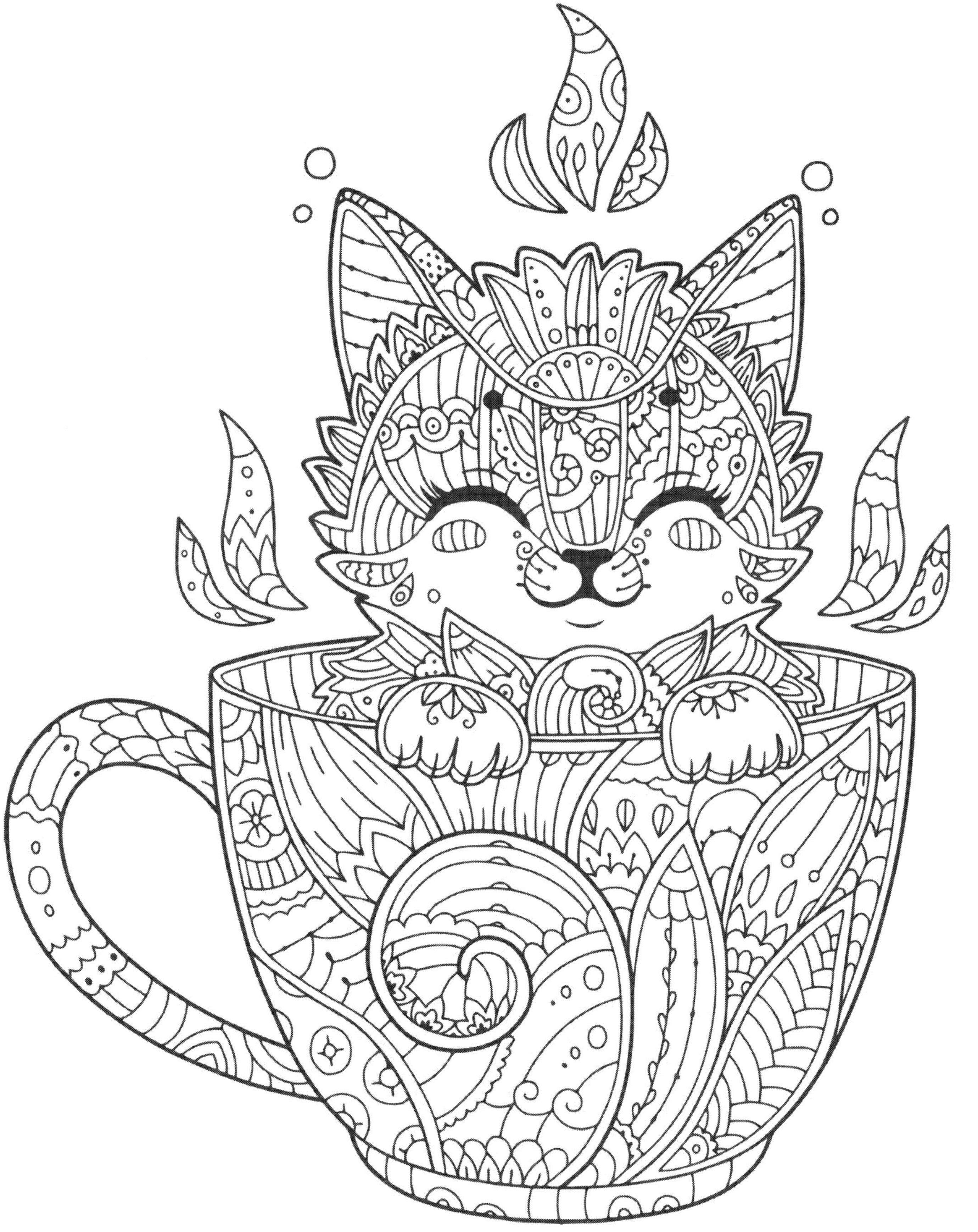

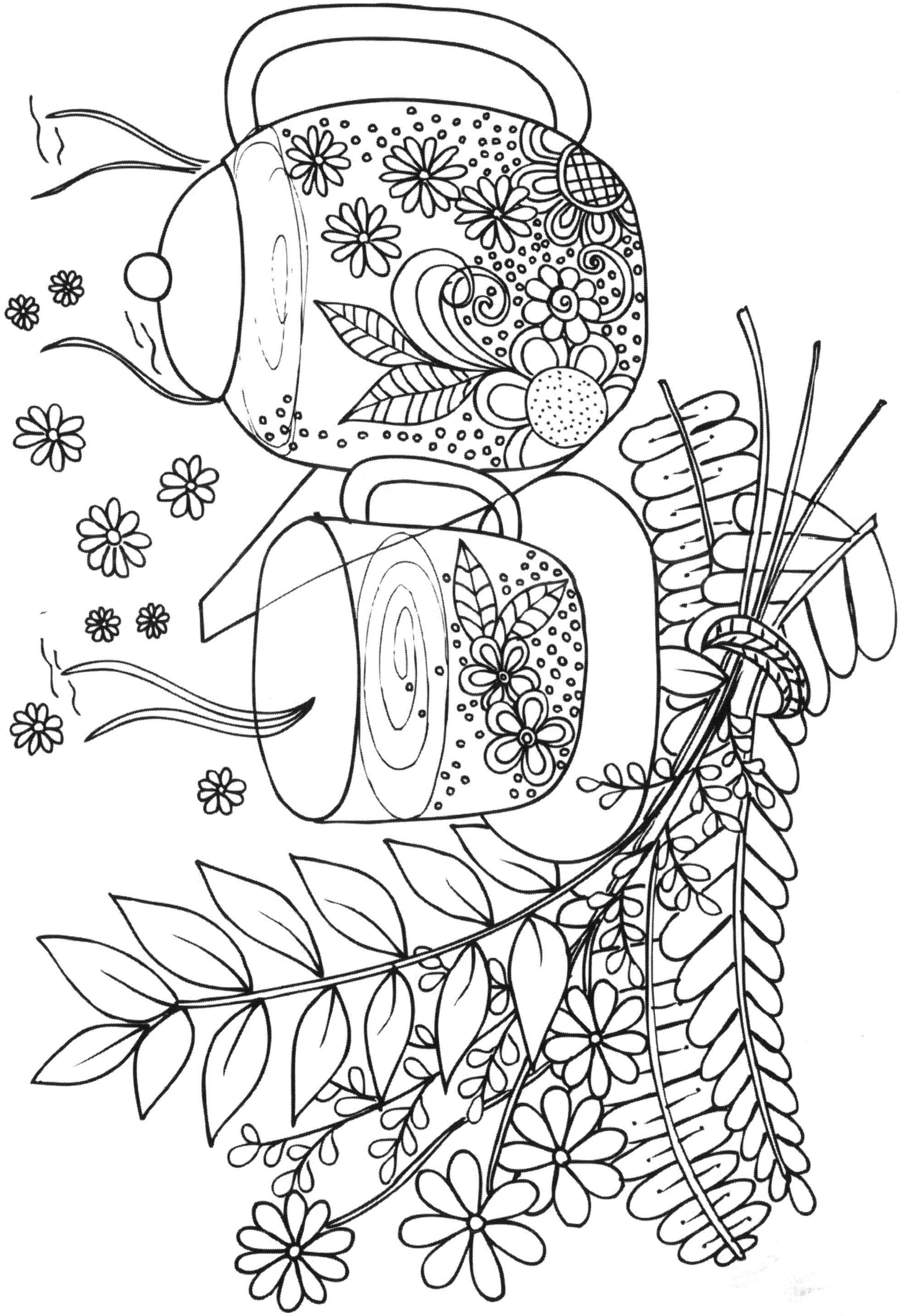

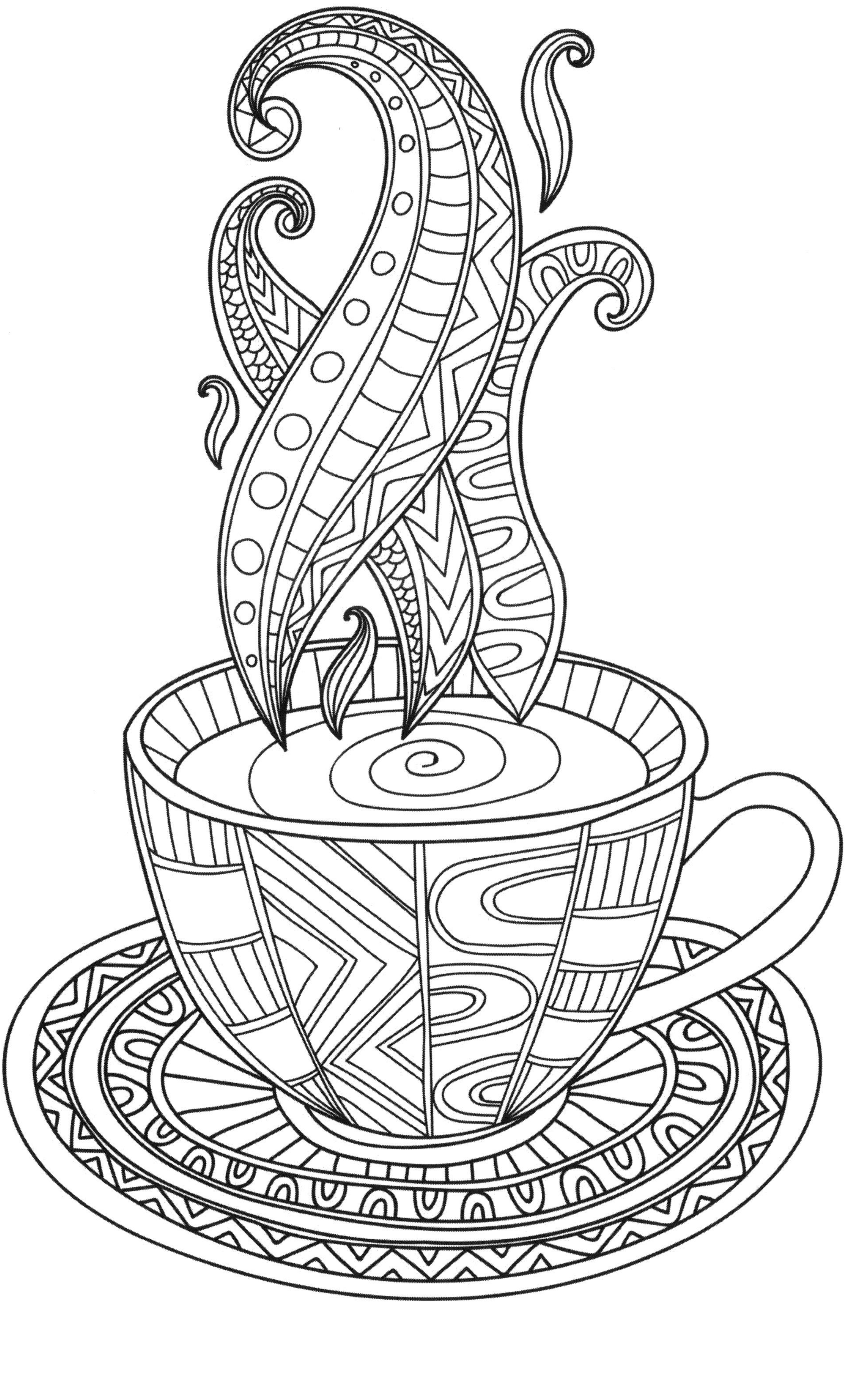

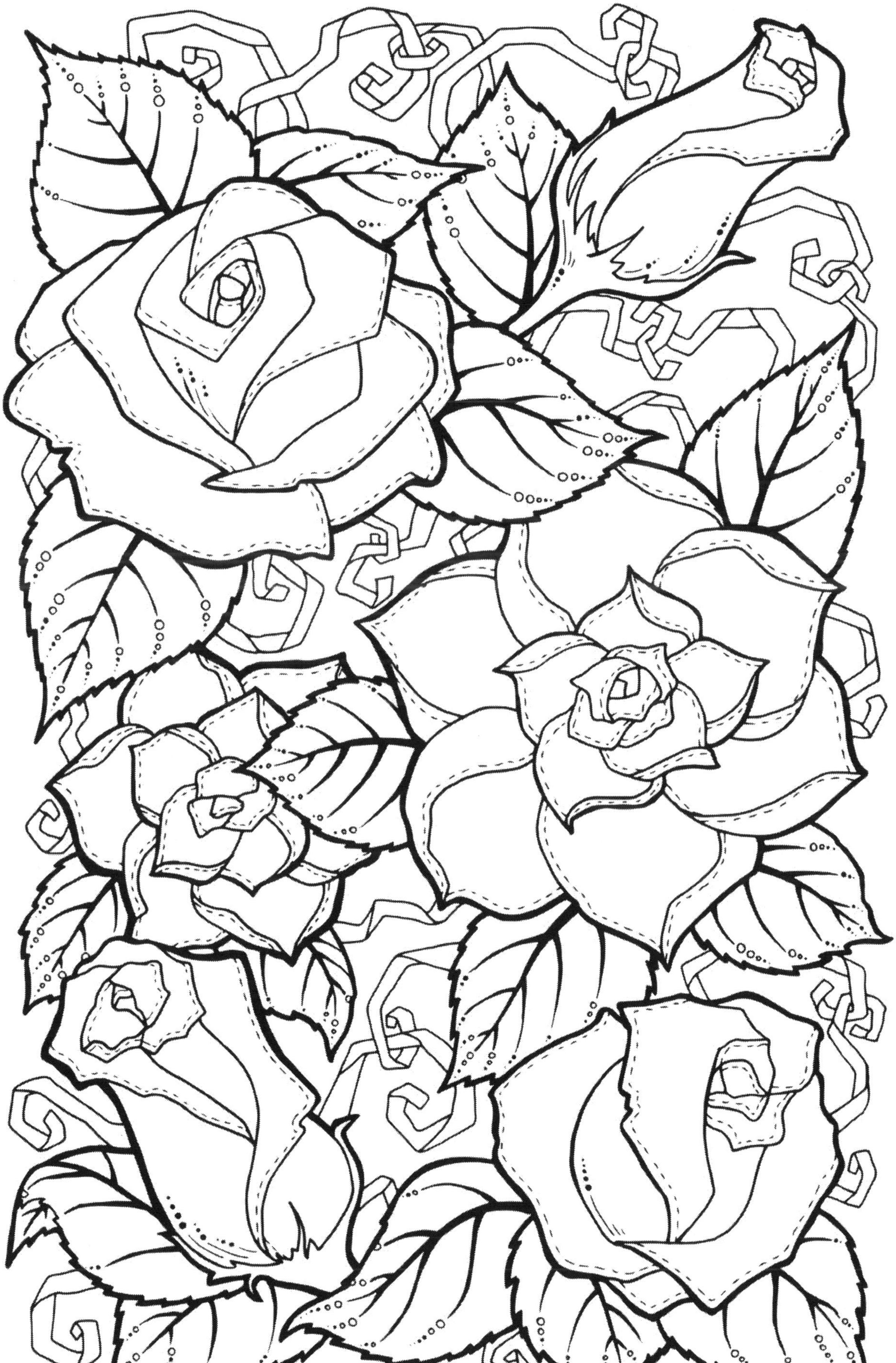

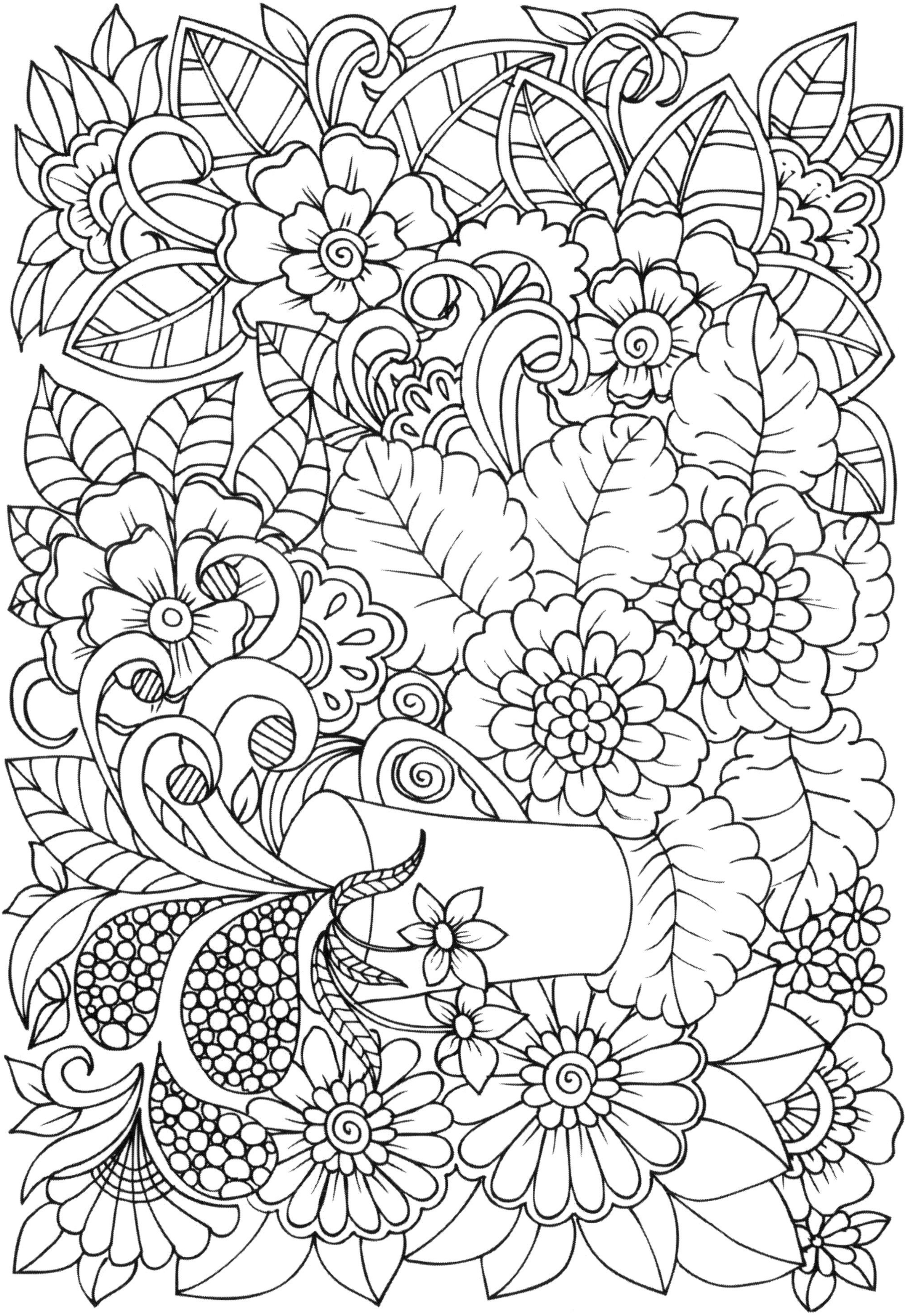

35770217R00031

Made in the USA
Middletown, DE
08 February 2019